NEW ZEALAND

Lyn Larson

Lerner Publications • Minneapolis

Lerner Publications Company
A division of Lerner Publishing Group, Inc.
241 First Avenue North
Minneapolis, MN 55401 USA

For reading levels and more information, look up this title at www.lernerbooks.com.

Library of Congress Cataloging-in-Publication Data

Larson, Lyn.
        New Zealand / by Lyn Larson.
            p.   cm. — (Country explorers)
        Includes index.
        ISBN: 978–0–7613–6413–9 (lib. bdg. : alk. paper) —
ISBN: 978–0–7613–7214–1 (EB pdf)
        1. New Zealand—Juvenile literature. I. Title.
    DU408.L37 2011
    993—dc22   2010018957

Manufactured in the United States of America
2 – DOC – 8/1/15

Table of Contents

AUSTRALIA

TASMANIA
(AUSTRALIA)

Welcome!

Every day is a good day in New Zealand. People greet one another by saying "G'day." This beautiful country is in the South Pacific Ocean. It lies halfway between the equator and the South Pole. (The equator is a line that goes around Earth's middle.) New Zealand has two main islands, the North Island and the South Island. Many smaller islands surround them. New Zealand's nearest neighbor is Australia.

New Zealand is known for its beautiful mountains and waterways.

equator

New
Zealand

South
Pole

TASMAN
SEA

NEW
ZEALAND

NORTH
ISLAND

Auckland

Hamilton

WAIKATO
R.

Whakarewarewa

MT.
NGAURUHOE

MT.
TONGARIRO

MT.
TARANAKI

LAKE
TAUPO

WANGANUI
R.

MT.
RUAPEHU

RANGITIKEI
R.

Wellington

SOUTH
PACIFIC OCEAN

MILES

0   50   100   150

0   50   100   150

KILOMETERS

Greymouth

WAIRAU
R.

SOUTHERN ALPS

Milford Sound

Christchurch

WAITAKI
R.

SOUTH
ISLAND

CLUTHA
R.

Dunedin

mountains

volcano

country's capital

city

Mount Ngauruhoe and Mount Ruapehu are active volcanoes at the center of the North Island.

Across the Land

Volcanoes formed the North Island. Some volcanoes there are still active. That means the volcanoes can still push out smoke and lava. In areas near volcanoes, heated water bubbles in hot springs. Hot water shoots out from geysers.

Tall, rocky mountains run along the South Island. They are the Southern Alps. Glaciers (large ice masses) top some mountain peaks. Rain forests lie west of the mountains. A plains region stretches along the east side.

Map Whiz Quiz

Take a look at the map on page 5. Trace the outline of New Zealand onto a sheet of paper. Look for the Tasman Sea. Mark this side of your map with a *W* for west. Find the South Pacific Ocean. Mark this side with an *E* for east. Above the North Island, put an *N* for north. Put an *S* for south below the South Island. Color New Zealand green. Color the ocean and sea blue.

The South Island's rain forests receive about 200 inches (508 centimeters) of rain each year. In some areas, walkways help hikers move easily through the forest.

Water, Water Everywhere

Do you like being by water? Then New Zealand is for you! The Pacific Ocean surrounds the country. To the west lies the Tasman Sea, part of the Pacific Ocean.

The bright blue waters of the Tasman Sea splash against the west coast of the South Island.

Lake Taupo is New Zealand's largest lake. It formed inside the crater of an old volcano. The country's longest river is the Waikato on the North Island. On the South Island, the Clutha and Waitaki rivers start in mountain lakes.

The Waikato River travels 264 miles (425 kilometers) through the North Island's rolling hills.

Seasons

New Zealand lies south of the equator. The seasons there are opposite from those in countries north of the equator. New Zealand's summer months are December, January, and February. Winter months are June, July, and August.

These people enjoy a January day at a beach near Dunedin, on the South Island.

New Zealanders enjoy mild weather with lots of sunshine. Winds blowing across the Tasman Sea bring moisture. More rain falls on the west side of the islands than on the east side. Snow usually falls only in the mountains.

Shaky Earth

About fifteen thousand earthquakes shake the area around New Zealand each year. Most are too small to notice. But people feel some of them.

11

Wild weather and waves hit the west coast of the South Island.

Animal Life

Millions of years ago, mainly birds lived on the islands. Some stayed on the ground. Over time, they lost their ability to fly. Birds like the kiwi and the kakapo have become endangered. Fewer than 125 kakapos are still living.

This kakapo (*left*) stretches its wings. A kiwi (*above*) sits among ferns in the forest. Neither of these endangered birds can fly.

Other New Zealand animals include the giant weta. It measures about 4 inches (10 cm) long. That makes it one of the world's largest insects. The tuatara is the country's largest reptile. It has a row of spiny plates on its back.

Many Meanings for Kiwi

Many New Zealanders think of the kiwi bird as a symbol for the country. New Zealanders even call themselves Kiwis. New Zealanders also named a fruit after the bird. Kiwi fruit is green inside. But the outside is brown and fuzzy, just like the kiwi bird.

The giant weta is so heavy that it cannot jump. It moves slowly in trees or on the forest floor.

First People

The Maori were the first humans to live on these islands. Maori explorers traveled here by canoe. They came from faraway Pacific islands. Starting about seven hundred years ago, Maori tribes lived on the main islands.

For hundreds of years, Maori tribes were the only people living on the islands that became New Zealand.

European explorers came later. The Dutch explorer Abel Tasman sailed near the islands in 1642. In 1769, British captain James Cook made maps of the area. Soon more Europeans arrived to hunt seals and whales.

Naming the New Country

The first Maori explorers named the islands *Aotearoa*, meaning "Land of the Long White Cloud." The Maori still use this name. The name New Zealand came from Dutch mapmakers after Tasman's voyage.

Captain James Cook of Great Britain made three trips to explore the Pacific Ocean.

Modern People

More than 4 million people live in New Zealand. Most people have European backgrounds. Their ancestors came from countries such as England, Ireland, Germany, Italy, and the Netherlands.

New Zealanders with European backgrounds cheer at a music festival.

About three out of every twenty people have Maori backgrounds. The Maori culture is important to all New Zealanders.

Ties to Britain

New Zealand became a British territory in 1840. Ever since, it has had strong ties to Britain. Modern-day New Zealand runs its own government. But Queen Elizabeth II of Britain is also New Zealand's queen.

A Maori dance group performs songs from their culture.

17

North Island Cities

A quarter of all Kiwis live in Auckland, the biggest city on the North Island. Many businesses have offices in downtown skyscrapers. People living here like to go sailing or boating. People call Auckland the City of Sails.

Queen Street in Auckland is a busy shopping area. In New Zealand, cars drive on the left side of the road.

Steep hills surround Wellington, New Zealand's capital. Many people here work for the government. The main government building is called the Beehive. This unusual, round building stands about 100 feet (about 30 meters) high.

Dear Grandma and Grandpa,
Today we're visiting Whakarewarewa. It's a funny name! You say it like this: "fa-ka-ree-wa-ree-wa." Volcanoes are nearby. The water underground is very hot. We've seen steamy hot springs and bubbling mud pools. Boiling water shot way up into the air from a geyser! See you soon!

Love,
Anika

Whakarewarewa

South Island Sites

The South Island has fewer people than the North Island. Christchurch is the largest city. Parks and playgrounds are plentiful. Many Kiwis here have beautiful gardens.

Christchurch Botanic Gardens is a beautiful place to visit in spring. Here, colorful tulips bloom near a flowering tree.

Smaller towns dot the rest of the island. Kiwis and tourists alike enjoy outdoor activities in the mountains and along the coasts. Green farmland runs through the center of the island.

Tourists speed through Milford Sound on the South Island.

Family Life

How big is your family? In New Zealand, families are usually small. Most parents have just one or two children. Many families spend time together outdoors. They may plant gardens. And they might cook meals on the barbie. That's the Kiwi word for grill.

Families enjoy picnics at a park near Auckland.

Most Maori families live in cities, just like other Kiwis do. The Maori word for family is *whanau*. Family ties are important to them. Some Maori can trace their family connections back to the first people who came to the islands.

A Maori girl smiles with her father.

City Living and Country Living

Most New Zealand families live in cities. They have homes with small gardens. Usually, kids have their own bedrooms. Many homes do not have furnaces. Families use small, portable heaters when it's cold at night.

This cozy neighborhood in Auckland is filled with comfortable homes and quiet streets.

Some families live on farms. Parents and kids work hard raising animals such as dairy cattle, beef cattle, or deer. Many farm families have sheep herds. Sheep provide wool, milk, and meat. Farm kids also work in crop fields or tend fruit orchards.

Farms Are Important

People around the world enjoy meat, wool, and dairy products from New Zealand. Many fruit crops also go to stores overseas. Farmers grow citrus fruits, apples, nectarines, peaches, berries, avocados, and kiwi fruit.

Some South Island families live on farms. Their animals graze on the rich grassland.

Eating Well

New Zealanders enjoy many foods. The main meats are lamb, venison (deer meat), fish, and shellfish. Cooks use sweet potatoes in lots of dishes. Fresh fruit tops a favorite dessert called pavlova.

Pavlova is a dessert with a crisp outside and marshmallow-like inside. Kiwis often serve it for holidays.

During a Maori gathering called a *hangi*, people cook food over hot rocks in a pit in the ground. The cooks pile up baskets of meat, vegetables, and dessert on the hot rocks. They cover the pile with wet cloths and then dirt. In three hours, the food is ready to dig up and eat.

A Maori man shows a group of tourists how to cook food during a hangi.

27

Getting Around

Most New Zealand families own cars. People there drive on the left side of the road. Streets have roundabouts (traffic circles) instead of four-way stops at corners. Ferries carry people and cars between the North Island and the South Island.

Large ferries travel between the main islands several times a day. They carry cars and people across the water.

Many people fly from one part of the country to another. New Zealand has more than one hundred airports. A train system also helps people get around.

People board trains at a station in Auckland.

Schooltime

Do you go to school all year long? Kiwi kids do. Their school year starts at the end of January. Students have two-week breaks in April, July, and October. They have six weeks off from mid-December to the end of January. This is their summer vacation.

It's recess at this elementary school in Greymouth, on the South Island.

Kiwi kids go to school from the age of five to the age of nineteen. They take classes in math, science, social studies, and technology. Students also study English and Maori. Some schools teach most of their classes in the Maori language.

A teacher shows a picture book to these elementary schoolchildren during an outdoor lesson.

Two National Languages

Since 1987, the Maori language and English have been the country's official spoken languages. The Maori alphabet has only fifteen letters. Their words use many vowels.

A teacher leads a Maori language class.

Kiwi English sounds different from American English. Kiwis also use some words from British English. Here are a few Kiwi words and their meanings.

SLOW DOWN!
PENGUINS CROSSING

KIA TUPATO!
HE KORORĀ   WHITI A

This sign, in English and Maori, warns drivers about penguins crossing the road.

33

Religion

More than half of New Zealanders are Christian. Most Christians are Protestants or Roman Catholics. About one-third of the population does not belong to any religious group.

The Christchurch Cathedral is the most visited church building in New Zealand. More than 700,000 people tour it each year.

The Maori have their own religion. They believe that a spirit lives in all things. Respect for all people is important. In modern times, most Maori have blended their native religion with Christianity.

Wood carvings decorate a Maori meeting house. People use these buildings for weddings, funerals, and important gatherings.

Celebrate!

Do you celebrate the New Year? Most Kiwis celebrate January 1 with parties and fireworks. The Maori also have a New Year party in June. They celebrate when the constellation (group of stars) Matariki appears during the first new moon.

ANZAC Day on April 25 is a national holiday. ANZAC stands for Australian and New Zealand Army Corps. On this day, New Zealanders remember the military people who served in World War I (1914–1918).

The Maori fly huge kites during the Matariki (New Year) festival in June.

Touching Noses

The *hongi* is a special Maori greeting. *Hongi* means "to embrace." During the greeting, people press their noses together. The Maori do this to exchange *ha* (the breath of life) with one another.

Two Maori men exchange a hongi greeting.

37

Art, Books, and Movies

Maori artists often use traditional designs in their works. Some carve wood, bone, and soft stone with swirling patterns. Their artworks often tell stories and feature faces and bodies of people.

Moko (Maori tattooing) is a popular art form. Artists use ink to cover men's faces and bodies with swirling patterns. On women, artists usually tattoo only the chin and lips.

38

Kiwis are known for books and movies. Author Witi Ihimaera's book *The Whale Rider* became a movie. Peter Jackson, a native New Zealander, filmed *The Lord of the Rings* movies there.

The Lord of the Rings movies were filmed in many locations around New Zealand.

Music and Dance

Do you enjoy music? Kiwi musicians perform all kinds of music. Hip-hop, reggae, pop, and rock music are popular. Some artists blend modern music with more traditional Maori music.

Ladyhawke is a popular singer and songwriter who was born in New Zealand.

The Maori have a special performance called a *haka*. Men and women chant, sing, and act out a song. They clap, slap their bodies, yell, and leap into the air. The Maori dance a haka to celebrate, to mourn, or to challenge an enemy.

Maori dancers perform a haka at an arts festival.

Sports and Activities

What's your favorite team sport? Most Kiwis would pick rugby. Players kick and run a ball toward the other team's goal. New Zealand's national team is the All Blacks.

The New Zealand All Blacks are one of the best rugby teams in the world.

Many people enjoy skiing and snowboarding in the mountains. Water lovers go white-water rafting and jet boating on rivers. They also like surfing and sailboat racing on the ocean.

In 1987, A. J. Hackett and Henry Van Asch invented bungee jumping. Jumpers strap on a harness with rubber cords. The cords attach to a bridge or other structure. When people jump, they free fall hundreds of feet. But the strong cords keep them from crashing into the ground.

Bungee jumping is an exciting sport that started in New Zealand.

43

THE FLAG OF NEW ZEALAND

New Zealand's flag has a dark blue background. The Union Jack—the British flag—is in the upper left quarter. It reminds New Zealanders of their connection to Great Britain. On the right side of the flag are four red stars outlined in white. The stars are in the shape of a constellation called the Southern Cross. Only people south of the equator can see this constellation.

FAST FACTS

FULL COUNTRY NAME: New Zealand

AREA: 103,089 square miles (267,000 square kilometers), or about as big as the state of Colorado

MAIN LANDFORMS: the mountain ranges Southern Alps, Ngauruhoe, Ruapehu, Taranaki, and Tongariro; active and inactive volcanoes; coastal plains; rain forests; and 142 small islands

MAJOR RIVERS: Clutha, Rangitikei, Waikato, Wairau, Waitaki, and Wanganui.

ANIMALS AND THEIR HABITATS: kaka, kakapo (rain forests and grasslands); Archey's frog, Hamilton's frog, kiwi, Maud Island frog (forests, scrub, swamps, grasslands); kea, short-tailed bats (forests); black stilt/kaki, brown teal/pateke, Hochstetter's frog (rivers and wetlands); albatross, elephant seals, fjordland crested penguin, katipo spider, New Zealand sea lion, tiny blue penguin, tuatara, Westland petrel/taiko, yellow-eyed penguin (ocean coasts); humpback whales, Maui's and Hector's dolphins, marlin, orca whales, pilot whales, sharks, sperm whales, tuna (oceans); geckos, long-tailed bats, skinks, weta (throughout)

CAPITAL CITY: Wellington

OFFICIAL LANGUAGES: English, Maori

POPULATION: about 4,213,420

GLOSSARY

ancestor: a relative who lived long ago

earthquake: the shaking of the ground caused by the shifting of underground rock

endangered: in danger of dying off completely

equator: an imaginary line that circles Earth at the middle. It divides the world into a north half and a south half.

ferry: a boat used to carry goods, vehicles, and people

geyser: a hole in Earth where hot water and steam sometimes shoot up

island: a piece of land surrounded by water

map: a drawing or chart of all or part of Earth or the sky

mountain: a part of Earth's surface that rises into the sky

volcano: an opening in Earth's surface through which hot, melted rock and gases shoot up

TO LEARN MORE

BOOKS

Jackson, Barbara. *New Zealand.* Washington, DC: National Geographic, 2008. Check out more details about this country's history, natural environment, government, and economy.

Mattern, Joanne. *Crazy Creatures of Australia and New Zealand.* Logan, IA: Perfection Learning, 2001. Learn about the interesting mammals, birds, insects, and marine life in New Zealand and its neighboring country, Australia.

McCollum, Sean. *Australia.* Minneapolis: Lerner Publications Company, 2008. Tour the neighboring country of Australia in this fun title.

Strudwick, Leslie. *Maori.* New York: Weigl Publishers, 2005. Learn more about New Zealand's first people, the Maori.

WEBSITES

All Blacks
http://files.allblacks.com/onlinemediaguide/media/video/05_kapaopango_match.wmv
Watch a video of New Zealand's All Blacks rugby team doing a haka before a match.

Korero Maori
http://www.korero.maori.nz/forlearners/basics/lessons/index.html
Hear how to pronounce words and phrases in Maori.

National Geographic Kids
http://kids.nationalgeographic.com/Places/Find/New-zealand
Explore New Zealand through pictures and videos at this site from *National Geographic Kids.*

INDEX